Purchased at pastor's retreat

Lavon

Herbert Garrett Jr

1959

Dover Memorial Library
Gardner-Webb University
P.O. Box 836
Boiling Springs, N.C. 28017

PRIVATE LIBRARY OF

Herbert C. Garrett Jr.

NO..............................

"And please return it. You may think this a strange request, but I find that although many of my friends are poor arithmeticians, they are nearly all of them good book-keepers."—Scott.

School of Divinity

Gardner-Webb University
School of Divinity

This book donated
by

Dr. Herbert Garrett, Jr

"THAT I MAY KNOW HIM"

Books by Vance Havner

That I May Know Him
Jesus Only
Pleasant Paths
It Is Time!
By the Still Waters
Peace Like a River
Consider Him
Rest Awhile
Road to Revival
The Secret of Christian Joy

"That I May Know Him"

A Personal Testimony

By

VANCE HAVNER

NEW YORK

Fleming H. Revell Company

LONDON AND GLASGOW

BX
6495
.H288
A3

Copyright, MCMXLVIII, by

FLEMING H. REVELL COMPANY

Printed in the United States of America

New York 10: 158 Fifth Avenue
London, E.C. 4: 29 Ludgate Hill
Glasgow, C.2: 229 Bothwell Street

FOREWORD

*"Here I raise mine Ebenezer;
Hither by Thy help I'm come."*

THIS BOOK is not an effort at autobiography. Rather, it is a testimony to that grace which has brought me safe thus far, and will, I am persuaded, lead me home.

It is difficult to write such an account. There is no way to escape the personal pronoun. But it is the writer's sincere hope that through the meanderings of the story the reader may discern chiefly and be most aware of the Unseen Presence. In this little book I would, like Samuel of old, set up a stone and say, "Hitherto hath the Lord helped us." And being assured of the Hitherto, we fear not the Henceforth.

V. H.

Greensboro, N.C.

CONTENTS

I

"TRAIN UP A CHILD . . ."

IN THE RED HILLS of North Carolina's Catawba County, between the little towns of Hickory and Shelby, rises one lookout that commands a glorious view of east and west, so striking that passing travelers often stop to look awhile. On the east, the woods and fields stretch to a level skyline, where at night the lights of five towns twinkle like footlights of a mammoth stage. On the west, the hills rise higher until they become the Blue Ridge Mountains, standing like calm and faithful sentinels along the far horizon.

To a little country boy who played among the oaks that circled his humble home on this high hilltop the eastern towns and twinkling lights seemed to speak of man's achievement, of progress and civilization, while the western hills seemed always to bear witness to nature and things eternal. The constant change of the one was balanced by the steady permanence of the other.

My home community was called Jugtown. It had every right to the title. My father and grandfathers and uncles were potters, and as a boy I often stood entranced while watching the wonder of clay growing into form and beauty under the deft hands of the

9

"worker on the wheels." From Jeremiah's lesson of the vessel marred and remade, preachers have prepared sermons on "A Life Made Over" or "The Divine Potter," and, with Paul, they have dwelt on God's sovereignty in making of the same lump one vessel to honour and another to dishonour. When nowadays we sing, "Have Thine own way, Lord, have Thine own way; Thou art the Potter, I am the clay," my thoughts go back to Jugtown and the fashioner of earthen vessels.

The home of my father, Pinkney (or, as the neighbours called him, "Pink") Havner was no pretentious affair. There were no rugs, no upholstered chairs, absolutely no modern conveniences. But in it and around it were all those simple and blessed things that made up the life of a country boy in that era just before progress got into high gear and, to use the clever phrase of another, before "the family was let out by auto and the world let in by radio." There was a plain house in healthful hilltop atmosphere; the best drinking water for miles around, good solid food that stuck to the ribs better than drugstore luncheons and modern nick-nacks with goofy names. There were woods to ramble in, with a spring and a brook in the pasture. On the back porch a honeysuckle vine lured the hummingbird, and each summer evening the wood thrush sang his vespers just about "milking time."

Father was the old-fashioned sort who believed that the authority in the home belonged to the parents and not to the children. He was in favour of the posterior application of superior force when necessary. Although he was called to preach, he never preached, and for the rest of his life he was conscious of having missed God's best. But he stood head and shoulders above most of the community, and the neighbours sought him often for counsel. Leader in the little country church, Corinth Baptist, he was the pastor's right-hand man, and his home was the haven of all itinerant preachers. I counted no privilege greater than to be allowed to sit up late when the minister spent the night with us and listen to him and father discourse on the things of God. Father knew the speech of Zion, the language of things heavenly. I marvel today that so many who claim to be Christians can talk on other subjects with liberty but are speechless concerning what ought to be their favourite theme. It was not so with father. Recently a friend of his said to me, "I do not remember ever talking with him over fifteen minutes before he turned the conversation to some spiritual subject." He could talk it, and, by the grace of God, he lived it. He had not only a talking but a "walking" knowledge of the Scriptures.

Father had a helpmeet in mother, a "keeper at home" who found there enough to do. Sturdy, practical, faithful, mother did not exercise herself in things too wonderful for her. She knew her orbit and stayed in it. In the lowly, simple duties of day-by-day she excelled, and her children call her blessed. Mother had little to say, but when the time came to size up a situation and pass her verdict she could do so very adequately! Father was sometimes inclined to take himself too seriously, and it was well that mother had a philosophy mixed with humour that stood her in good stead through many a troubled hour.

Into such an old-fashioned home this scribe was born on the seventeenth of October, 1901. Being a late arrival, much younger than his brother and sister, he had no playmates. Being extremely frail, he was fed for some years on a diet that would have kept him so had he not got hold of a bowl of cabbage one day when nobody was looking. He devoured that and because he survived, it was decided that probably he could stand any food if cabbage wouldn't kill him.

So he grew up in that leisurely good era, the last years of the horse-and-buggy age, before the modern hurricane set in. What happy recollections filter back from those hill-billy days of the old parlour lamp and the big family album, cotton-pickings and corn-shuckings, cornbread and milk at night and molasses in the morning, "singin's" on Sunday afternoons when the young folk gathered around the organ; the singing school where we learned the *do-re-mis* in shaped notes; the "big meetin'" at Corinth in August after "laying-by" time on the farm; commencement day, always called "the exhibition," at the little country school; the Old Soldiers' Reunion Day, the annual pink-lemonade event, at Newton, the county seat; the rocking chair before the old fireplace, cozy retreat on many a snowy day; tramping the summer woods with Shep, faithful companion of boyhood years—no man has fully lived who did not grow up with a dog!

Happy dear old days among old-timey people back

in the hills! There were woods aplenty to walk in. Sawmills had not yet devastated the timber, and one could start out in almost any direction and soon lose himself among the oaks and pines. I remember a character we used to call "'Possum John." He lived by hunting and fishing and a little farming. He could see a hiding rabbit where the rest of us saw only a clump of grass. What a simple life he lived, wise in the ways of the woods! He was a sort of "white Indian" and seemed perennially happy. He hunted rabbits by day and 'possums by night, and was a sage in the lore of the woods and fields.

The memory which lingers most clearly and which, doubtless, means most is that of a few good books. I can remember reading *Pilgrim's Progress* to mother on winter nights. Christian and Christiana and Great-Heart and Faithful and all that immortal host that Bunyan gave to the world, how we grew tense over their tribulations and thrilled over their triumphs! How we enjoyed seeing the saints get safely over the river and into the Celestial City! In this day of peanut-butter-sandwich theology, what a price we have paid for passing up the moral beefsteak of books that are books indeed! Forget the sawdust and shavings of modern best-sellers and read *Pilgrim's Progress* again; then read Alexander Whyte's *Bunyan Characters* and add iron to your soul and muscle to your spiritual biceps!

Foxe's *Book of Martyrs* also claimed a share of my attention in those days. Somewhere Father had acquired a set of volumes, extracts from the best of literature. I revelled in *Little Women* and followed Alice on her trip *Through the Looking Glass,* becoming so enamoured of Looking-Glass Land that I devoutly wished I could get through the mirror on our best dresser and explore the strange world beyond.

But chiefest of all was the good old Book, to which I was encouraged to give first place. Aided by a book of Bible pictures and stories, I learned early that no characters can be so entrancing as Joseph and Moses and David and Elijah and Peter and Paul. I remember sitting with my cousins, going through the Bible pictures, labelling Cain bad and Abel good, and so through the book, dividing the sheep from the goats. For this generation, brought up on movie thrillers and silly comics, I covet a childhood nurtured on the Word of God. It might seem the depth of boredom to a modern youngster fed up on trash and jaded from worn-out excitements, but life was happier before the Amen age gave way to the era of So What.

II

"PREACH THE WORD . . ."

IT WAS "BIG MEETIN'" time at old Corinth, and I was
about ten years of age. We always had our "protracted
meeting" at Corinth the last week of July, and the
Methodists started theirs when ours ended. You would
have thought nobody could get saved except during the
last of July, for the date never varied. My grandmother
used to shout her way through both meetings—the
denomination didn't make much difference if you "got
happy."

I do not think anything in the preacners sermons
had particularly impressed me. But an accumulation
of influences was bearing on my heart. My father's
concern, my own reflections, the revival atmosphere—
through all these the Spirit spoke. Alone in the woods
below our house I knelt one afternoon and took Christ
as my Saviour. I do not remember what I said, but,
although in later years I was led to doubt for a while
the genuineness of that experience, I now feel that I
came to the Lord as best I knew, and I believe He received me.

A. C. Dixon, the great preacher of a generation ago,
grew up in a county adjoining mine. As a boy I
preached in many of the churches his preacher father

served before my day. Young Clarence Dixon had read *Pilgrim's Progress* and then found himself in a miserable state. He could not get his burden to suit him. It would not get big enough or heavy enough. He cried because he couldn't cry, was burdened because he wasn't burdened, depressed because he wasn't depressed. Finally, in a meeting where his father had preached on "What Must I Do To Be Saved?" he went forward and was kneeling there when his father came and asked how it was with him. "I believe on the Lord Jesus Christ," young Clarence replied. His father assured him that it was as simple as that, and A. C. Dixon said later, "There was no ecstatic joy. I began simply by resting on Christ and His promises."

My experience was somewhat similar, except that I remember running back to where my father was at work in an old shop. I went in through the window and he sensed at once that something had happened. We embraced each other in what was a most unusual outburst of joy since we were not given to emotional demonstration. That night we went up to the church for the evening meeting, and father related my experience to the pastor and evangelist. On a following Sunday I was baptized with others in the summer "baptizing" in South Fork River.

I remember setting up a stone in the woods to mark the scene of my conversion. Perhaps there was undue veneration for a spot of ground and maybe something of the spirit of Naaman and his load of dirt. Of course, I learned later that Elbethel is greater than Bethel, that the God of the place is more important than the place. But in this age of indefinite experience, with the saints living in ethical fogs and moral twilights, it is well to have known a happy day that fixed one's choice, which by no means takes away any glory from Him, our Saviour and our God.

Diverse are the ways by which men come to Christ. And great is the temptation to judge others if they do not have mud put on their eyes and go to Siloam exactly as we did. There were years when I allowed the devil the luxury of worrying me because I did not have the vivid sort of experience that some spectacular sinner could relate. Thank God for all their stories, and I revel in their colourful accounts of Divine deliverance. But I have learned that the most amazing thing is the amazing grace that saves any and all who believe, and I am glad that God brought me to Himself when I had both the years and the spirit of a child.

One has to be doubly careful in preaching about conversion. It is true that there are those who trust in a false hope—professors but not possessors. There is a counterfeit conversion, for Satan imitates every work of grace. But we must beware lest, in endeavouring to arouse such souls from their carnal security, we upset humble believers who may be weak in faith but have yet truly leaned on Jesus for repose. Better a millstone around one's neck than so to offend such little ones who believe in Him. Blessed is that experience simple enough to keep one from overpainting his conversion, yet stirring enough to bring a sparkle to the eye each time he tells it.

My ventures in public speaking began with short talks in Sunday school. Presently two discourses were developed: one on the books of the Bible, a sort of running comment from Genesis to Revelation; another on "Periods of the Bible," a flying trip through Bible history. I was not quite twelve years of age when I was invited to speak on a Wednesday night in the First Baptist Church of Hickory, twelve miles from my home. A neighbour took me and my father there in his Ford. It was my second automobile ride—too much for one night. Eventually we arrived at the church. No structure has looked more imposing since! It seemed as if it were a mile to the pulpit. I remember telling father to pray for me. When it came my time to speak, I stood on a chair, while the pastor, J. D. Harte, stood on one side and the State Evangelist, W. R. Bradshaw, on the other. It was like Aaron and Hur holding up the hands of Moses!

So my ministry began. Of course, there were open doors. A twelve-year-old preacher was a novelty, and naturally attracted the curious. With father accompanying me and hiring a neighbour to take us each Sunday in his Ford, we journeyed to town and country churches for two and sometimes three services each Lord's Day. It was a task in those days, with dirt roads and automobiles that were certain to have at least one tire puncture or engine trouble before the day was over. If they had thirty horsepower at least twenty seemed to be dead! My messages turned into textual sermons. "Follow Me," "The Prodigal Son," "Prepare To Meet Thy God," "Behold The Lamb of God," "Arise, Let Us Be Going," and "Heaven" were favourites. My itineration covered the Piedmont section of North Carolina, extended a time or two to lower Virginia and upper South Carolina. No protracted meetings were held, few invitations were given. There linger memories of crowded churches, lines of handshakers, tiresome dusty or muddy trips, Sunday dinners and suppers in strange homes. The task seemed perfectly natural and was readily laid aside on Monday for a trip through the woods. There were, of course, those gushing souls who thought I was a prodigy. Nor was there any lack of critics who charged that father prepared my sermons and was the real inspiration of the work. How much good was done I do not know. God keeps the books. We were just a plain country father and a shy boy with a Bible. I view with concern today any precocious child, for there is a price to pay. My heart goes out to that odd youngster who travels a path different from that of the average. Quench not his spirit lest you be found fighting against God. Pray for him and hope for the best.

It was a year after I began preaching that I stood in the little home church on a Saturday afternoon and asked to be licensed to preach the Gospel. The certificate gives the date as September 20, 1914. That was a tender occasion, and I remember the mellow spirit of those lowly farmer folk, many of whom have since passed on, as they voted with full sympathy, believing the Lord had called me. I was only twelve, and those sturdy Baptists were not given to careless procedure with candidates for the ministry. They believed in being called to preach. Good character and honest intention and careful preparation they valued; but, over and above all that, they held that sometime, somewhere, young Samuel must hear the unmistakable Voice. Therefore, the full endorsement of the church greatly encouraged this young and timid Timothy. I have treasured the fellowship of old Corinth church through these years. It is a joy to return once in a while and preach in their new stone church that stands on the old hallowed ground. While it is true that our Lord said a prophet is not without honour save in his own country, it does not necessarilly follow that every preacher without honour at home is a prophet.

Three years after I was licensed to preach, I was ordained, and "did accordingly receive the full, entire and hearty approbation of the presbytery in my officially entering upon the work of the Gospel ministry, administering the ordinances of the Gospel and performing those duties and enjoying all those privileges to which a minister of Christ is called." This service in the same home church found me a rather nervous candidate, without theological training and not well prepared to answer some hard questions—about predestination, for instance. But the examining brethren were considerate, having passed through the same deep waters in the past. So, from being what the Methodists used to call an "exhorter," I passed into the field of a full-fledged minister. It has been said that a preacher takes a text and sticks to it, while an exhorter just sloshes around in it. I fear that my sloshing around did not end with my ordination, but I trust I am not one who pounds because he can't expound.

III

"STUDY . . ."

THE "BOY-PREACHER" days moved along, each Sunday bringing new crowds, new faces, new experiences. The week-days were spent at home. I recall several Sunday evenings in the First Baptist Church of Shelby, North Carolina, a Baptist stronghold. The crowds were the largest I had faced so far; I stood in the midst of the throng on a table and was more nervous about staying on the table than on account of the crowd. There was no stage fright during those years but plenty of it later.

Another memory is that of wearing my first white suit when I was preaching from a wagon to an outdoor crowd on a Fourth-of-July Sunday. Another is addressing an audience of men in the Y.M.C.A. of Spartanburg, South Carolina. Many country churches were visited. Whoever said, "If you are preaching in town, take your best clothes; if in the country, take your best sermon," did not speak unwisely. There was a deep delight in those days before cars and better roads had brought the city too close to preach to plain folk in plain garments, humble souls fresh from the soil, always close to things elemental. From the days of Him whom the common people heard gladly the Gospel has been best received by those of humblest station. Not many wise, mighty, and noble are called. If you would try out a preacher, send him to preach to farmers: if he cannot make the grade there, let him reconsider his call—or maybe he needs to be converted.

An indelible impression was made when my father took me to Charlotte to attend the meetings conducted by Dr. J. Wilbur Chapman and Charles M. Alexander. The radiant spirit of Charlie Alexander as he sang "A Little Talk With Jesus Makes It Right, All Right" and "Shine Where You Are" could not fail to capture a country boy out to preach the Gospel. And Dr. Chapman's gracious smile and the little Testament he gave me, which I treasure to this day, won my heart. Then there was the piano artistry of Harry Barraclough and Albert Brown's singing of "The Prodigal Son." I little dreamed then that in later years I would get to know Mr. Brown quite well and hear him sing in some of my own meetings.

I am glad that I came along in time to enjoy a little of the old-time evangelism that followed the great days of Moody. I wish I might have heard Moody, but I did hear Chapman and Torrey and Gypsy Smith and Billy Sunday. Instead of the churches uniting now for such a great endeavour, it is pretty difficult to get even one church united for meetings today!

The "boy-preacher" years merged into high-school years, for one must go to school some time. My education had been rather fragmentary—several irregular winter periods in the little two-teacher country school at home, the old-fashioned sort with the hand-bell that called us to "books"; the much-carved wooden desks, the dusty old blackboard painted on the wall, the tin dinner buckets, the pail of water from the spring. I have read of a coloured brother who thought to stave off contagious disease by buying a sanitary drinking cup and then having every member of the family use it! We drank from the same "dipper" in those school days, and germs must have been scarcer before the mouth-wash era or none of us would have lived to tell the tale. We walked to and from school in the pre-bus age, and every step of the way was marked by some youthful escapade. I got along in spelling and geography and history, but mathematics was the bane of my existence. I remember the Friday afternoon spelling matches and one outstanding event, when, in competing with a near-by school, I went down in defeat on "quadrilateral."

Came the day when I loaded my belongings in a cheap trunk and journeyed in the old buggy over to Maiden, North Carolina, to enter South Fork Institute, a Baptist boarding school then on its last legs. I did not turn out to be the star student a boy preacher was supposed to be. The boy in me had to come out some time and he began asserting himself in a lot of innocent mischief which was puzzling to those who expected me to act like fifty instead of fifteen.

I was seized with "bird-fever," a passion for bird study which has been a life-saver to many. At home I had always enjoyed tramping the woods, but at Maiden it became an absorbing interest that filled notebooks and study hours supposed to be given to Latin and algebra. Many a lecture on grammar failed utterly to register on ears attuned to a warbler in the trees outside. Cæsar's ups and downs in Gaul had no appeal for one heart that stirred more readily to the drumming of a yellowhammer than to all the wars of Rome.

Even father could not understand such a strange turn in my interests and he saw little to be gained from ever so much knowledge of thrushes and titmice. When a bird guide was sent "on approval" and decreed not to be worth a dollar, I copied the main points in it before the ten days of grace expired. But God through nature often acts in mysterious ways His wonders to perform, and He knows better than the best of us what even the birds can do to save us from drying up. Said Mark Rutherford: "Men should not be too curious in analysing and condemning any means which nature designs to save them from themselves, whether it be coins, old books, curiosities, fossils or butterflies."

I have tried many times since to put down on paper something of the sheer ecstasy of those happy days when every new bird discovered was a major thrill: the morning call of the flicker in springtime, the evening serenade of the wood thrush, my favourite to this day; the rare delight of identifying the indigo bunting, and the big day when I found my first Blackburnian warbler; tramping the snowy woods in winter, watching the nuthatches run head downward on the trees trunks while the chickadees, titmice, and a few kinglets gave a spark of life to the cold, calm landscape. My bird guide is filled with entries of new feathered acquaintances along with my own efforts to write down their songs. I remember the day after I returned home from my first term at boarding school: the apple trees were in bloom, the bees were hard at work, the air was full of calls and carols and trills and medleys, and I was a boy in the country! In these days of hotels and public parks I would gladly exchange most of the drummed-up excitements of this rackety age for the exuberance that tingled in every boyish nerve on a clear spring morning when I awoke to a bedlam of bird music back home on the farm.

The birds, however, did not keep me from making a passing grade at Maiden, from where I went to Boiling Springs High School, another Baptist institution in a country village. Dear old Professor Huggins, head of the school, and a man of God, readily caught on to my make-up and remarked later that anyone looking for me would find me either in the library or down the creek looking for birds. But Professor Huggins was a real soul who did not dry up teaching. In fact, more than one mathematics period slipped by with very little mathematics in it because the Professor got going on themes even more important, realising that students needed God more than they needed geometry. Those were stirring World War I days, when girls were coming to classes with tearful eyes because a brother or sweetheart had gone "over there." It was a fine time to drive home precious lessons, and Professor Huggins cast his bread on living waters.

Boiling Springs helped to rub off a little of my rusticity, although most of it has never disappeared, since the country cannot be taken out of the boy. I remember my first night there and how I watched my roommate, a city fellow, hang his expensive neckties over the dresser mirror. I had some ties of the twenty-five-cent variety and the contrast depressed me for some days, until I came across some immortal lines:

> "What tho' on hamely fare we dine,
> Wear hodden grey and a' that?
> Gie fools their silks, and knaves their wine—
> A man's a man for a'that!
> For a'that, and a'that,
> The honest man, tho' e'er sae poor,
> Is king o'men for a'that!"

During those days I learned to play the piano after a fashion, and what time the birds did not take from my studies the piano did. I was the pest of the music studio, always pestering the music teachers to play things too difficult for me. I could be lured in from any part of the campus by a few bars of Paderewski's *Minuet in G*.

It was at Boiling Springs that I had my first date with a girl, and it was on the same evening that I wore my first long-pants suit. It was about all I could do to manage both at once, for either was enough for a high-school crowd to magnify out of all proportion. Well, those were dear years, with all the tender intertwinings of laughter and tears, the silly and sublime; before life got set, full of danger and delight, crossroads where one turns easily toward victory or despair, years when youthful hearts take on impressions that eternity may never erase.

Somehow, the spiritual fires did not burn so brightly during those days. I preached occasionally, but there was a lull as though the preacher was marking time until the boy caught up. Some were surprised that I did not take all the honours, but, after all, I was no genius, and I am glad that birds and music and wholesome mischief and sweethearts and all the normal experiences of a boy's life got tangled up in mine. I might have blown up trying to be bigger than I was ever meant to be. If your Johnny shows signs of being a "boy wonder," do not take from him his boyhood. God gave it to him, and no earthly laurels can compensate for the loss of it. For do not the mighty sit in millionaires' mansions and presidents' chairs, willing to trade it all could they but turn time backward in its flight and go fishing again—barefoot boys with cheeks of tan?

IV

"THOU KNEWEST MY PATH"

From Boiling Springs I went to Catawba College, a
school of the Reformed Church, then located at Newton, N. C. Those were war days and a Training Corps
was formed in the college. Reveille aroused us each
morning, and how glad I was that I did not have to
hustle down those cold stairs for setting-up exercises in
the winter dawn! "Over There," "Tipperary," "There's
A Long, Long Trail A'Winding," and "Rose of No
Man's Land" filled the air. Overseas caps appeared,
and stars in the windows spoke of hearts heavy for a
boy somewhere in France.

I prepared an oration about the war. I missed the
orator's medal in Boiling Springs in a round of war
speeches, the winning speech being the only one that
wasn't on that subject! But I won at Catawba College
with a rouser about making the world safe for democracy that brings a smile now, after the blood and thunder of another World War has left less democracy than
ever!

I preached in Newton's First Baptist several Sundays
during the spring term. Birds and piano-playing still
absorbed a lot of college time. There was a revival of
sermon-writing. I remember one on Samson, which I

29

called "The Price of a Shave." There was another on "Can These Dry Bones Live?" which must have made the saints squirm. There must be a special reward in heaven for church people who are willing to let upstart preachers practice on them, patient souls who have been made guinea pigs for many a youthful pastor's experiments.

During the summer of 1919 I supplied the pulpit of old Corinth Church back home and baptized my first candidates in the same river where I had followed the Lord in obedience some years before. That fall I went away to Wake Forest College, the Baptist college of North Carolina. I did not stay long. I walked at night on the country roads and tried to write a novel after the fashion of the Harold Bell Wright stories so popular then. I wanted to get back to preaching and wrote my father telling him so. His answer I have kept to this day. He did not tell me to stay or leave but to decide it after much prayer. Much as he wanted me to follow the prescribed course, he was wise enough to know that perhaps the Lord might not will it so. A college professor who appeared at the station when I left for home warned me that I would regret it. I cannot say that I have regretted it, but, of course, I would not advise others to take the same course. What seemed boyish restlessness at the time I now feel to have been part of the Divine leading toward the type of ministry God had for me.

With the beginning of 1920, I set out again on the path of my heart's desire, itinerant preaching. There were several favourite haunts to which I returned again and again. One was Mt. Paran, a rural church in South Carolina, where I preached while visiting a lovely family, the Sepochs, out in the country. Mrs. Sepoch had a family of girls, so she made me her boy, and was indeed a mother to me. Another was Bostic, North Carolina, a little mountain town, where many homes were open to me and where I conducted many "protracted meetings" and played the piano for others. Then there was old Unity Presbyterian Church, near Davidson, North Carolina, where I held forth several times and was often a guest in the good home of Robert Graham, who lived near by. I mention these good friends because they will never know how much their love and hospitality meant to this roving preacher during those days. I was making my way through uncertain years, a lonesome fellow going through his teens and trying to find himself. These friends took me to their hearts and homes and believed the Lord had something for me. I trust I may never disappoint them, to say nothing of Him, and if any measure of success is attained, much credit, humanly speaking, will be due to some plain good Christians who helped me along.

I remember a two-weeks' meeting held with a Baptist church in Richmond, Virginia, during this period. In 1940 I received a card from a minister telling how God called him to preach during one of those services back in 1921. He waited a long time to tell me, but it was a welcome return of bread cast on waters long ago.

I made a trip to Roanoke, Virginia, to hear Billy Sunday. I discovered that not only Billy Sunday but the State Fair and Barnum and Bailey were holding forth that week! I could find no place to sleep that night but I heard Billy preach his famous sermon on "Forces That Win." In recent years I have become acquainted with Mrs. Sunday, and have visited in the Sunday home in Winona Lake. I have looked over the many souvenirs of those great days of evangelism and have never ceased to wonder at the mighty impact of the famous baseball evangelist on his generation. In this day of religious lavender and rosewater, not a few wiseacres are disposed to underestimate the preaching of Billy Sunday, but any man who lived during his heyday knows that he gave the devil more trouble in one week than many ultra-modern preachers could cause in a century.

We had another colourful evangelist down South who, during his prime, was one of my favourites. He was Baxter McLendon, popularly known as "Cyclone Mac." "Mac's" own personal appearance, his long hair, square jaw, handle-bar moustache, and eyes that fairly burned, would attract a crowd. But "Mac" could preach, and when he "got in a weaving way" the thunder roared and the lightning flashed. It was old-time camp-meeting preaching, lurid and vivid, sin black, hell hot, judgment certain, eternity long, and salvation free. My father loved it, and it stirred my own soul. In these days of pale pulpitism I would welcome a night under "Mac's" big tent when heaven and earth met and the Fire came down.

Under the influence of "Mac's" meetings I decided to go to Moody Bible Institute. I arrived there in October, unheralded. I recall that I blundered into the Women's Building first, and that when they steered me to the proper desk in another building, card in hand for registration, and the lady secretary reached for my card, I shook hands with her, thinking she meant to welcome me to the Institute! I remember how I started up to my room, blue and homesick, when, suddenly, the men students in their evening devotions broke loose singing "My Anchor Holds." I had never heard such soulful singing, and I began to perceive that they "had something."

The influence of the Institute was a permanent and abiding blessing. The earnest zeal of the students, their testimonies, the prayer life one ran into all over the place, the emphasis on the old Book and the old faith, the stream of God-anointed speakers who passed through and gave the cream of their messages—these I have never forgotten. Who could forget Dr. R. A. Torrey's address on "Moody As I Knew Him," or Grattan Guiness or Charles W. Abel, with their missionary appeals? William Jennings Bryan came along with his great testimony. And Dr. James M. Gray, then president of the Institute, brought his meaty expositions of the Word. Of course, today, when preachers are being taught in many quarters not to believe the Bible, it is natural that Moody Bible Institute should be regarded by some as the champion of an outmoded orthodoxy. But be not deceived: this West Point of Christian service is belting the globe with witnesses who still believe the Gospel. Thank God for this Chicago beehive, "the school that D. L. Moody founded."

I returned South, and after working awhile with the Billy Sunday Club in Spartanburg, South Carolina, I put a little notice in a Baptist paper stating that I was available for a pastorate. It fell under the eye of John Brown, a church clerk in Eastern North Carolina, member of Salem Baptist Church near Elizabeth City in the "potato country." He had been deluged with letters from preachers who, for their wife's health or for other reasons, felt that they needed a change; but he decided to give one more candidate a try, so he wrote to me. Thus began a friendship with this farmer philosopher that lasted through the years until his passing. Once in a while we meet someone in our earthly pilgrimage who talks our language a little better than anybody else. I have known many more learned and renowned characters, but I doubt that I have ever had better fellowship than while chatting with Farmer John back at the creek among the cypresses and watching the water birds flap lazily by. He was never in a hurry, and would stop plowing any time to lean over the fence and pass the time of day. Whenever we met, formal salutations were unnecessary: we simply took up the thread of thought where we had left off last and talked until a shower of rain or the sinking sun would drive us home.

V

"PREACH . . . THE PREACHING THAT
I BID THEE"

IT WAS IN FEBRUARY, 1924, that I preached my first sermon in Weeksville. My subject was "Pharisees," and I
marvel now that I ever received a call on such a sermon.
I bore down unmercifully on the saints, and it was not
at all the sort of pulpit effort to win over a board of
deacons or a pulpit committee. But they called me and
I began what turned out to be four periods of preaching
in Weeksville, covering about five years in all. Those
years, with the intervals between, covered a transition
in my life, and because of all the changes God wrought
through that time Weeksville holds a special place in
my affections. No people ever bore more graciously
with a preacher through unsettled years than those
friends in Salem Church. They endured my youthful
pastoral experiments and put up with a lot of personal
eccentricities. I did not visit as much as I should have
done. I did not have an automobile—I have never
owned a car to this day—and they grew accustomed to
passing me by on the country roads because I was out
meditating and did not want to ride. Through all my
stays in Weeksville I heard very little criticism. When
I left the church and described the field in the paper,

the pulpit committee was flooded with letters from preachers who wanted to be the next pastor. In fact, after reading my own write-up, I almost decided to call off my resignation! But I had not overpainted the situation and I am not surprised that pastors love to stay there.

My first stay at Weeksville lasted exactly one year. During that time my preaching took on a modernistic color. I was first attracted to the liberal position by the mild position of Henry Drummond. I read Dr. Frank Crane, popular essayist. His book, *Why I Am A Christian,* fell into my hands, and his approach seemed to promise a fresher view of the Christian life. It was new to me and sounded challenging and stirred my youthful enthusiasm. Other liberal writings added fuel to the flame, and I began to preach this "new light." It brought no conviction of sin but instead soothed consciences and gave the impression that man was more weak than wicked and needed culture rather than Calvary. I congratulated myself on the increased attendance at church, supposing it indicated progress as a preacher. But while many complimented me, there were no conversions.

After my first year at Weeksville I resumed my travelling ministry under the impression that I had a new message to preach. In appealing to "the modern mind" I was not aware that "the modern mind" is not very modern and not much mind. My preaching was of the "repent as it were and believe in a measure or you'll be lost to some extent" variety. I remember one sermon on

"Atmosphere": the title was not inappropriate for there was air aplenty in it and hot air at that. In 1927 I returned to Weeksville and throughout the summer spoke on Sunday nights in the high school. I was called to act as supply pastor at my old church again. During this time I wrote a column for *The Independent,* a weekly paper edited by W. O. Saunders, who wrote for several nationally known magazines and who was a freethinker. He paid me the first money I ever earned for writing and urged me to enter free-lance journalism. He was kind to me, and when I left Weeksville again he wrote in his editorial: "In a world of bluster, bluff and bunk, Vance Havner is one of the few genuine souls it has been my pleasure to know." I appreciated that word from him, but while I was honest I found that honesty is not enough. I was not in the will of the Lord. Some years later, after I had returned to the true message, Mr. Saunders published for me one article stating my return to the old position, though he did not share my convictions at all.

During those years of digression from the true purpose of my life I did learn one thing: I now know something of the processes of thought one goes through in embracing a liberal position. It is easy to detect in men or movements if one has been infected with it in the past. It is a subtle thing, into which one drifts almost imperceptibly. Of course, there is nothing new about liberalism. "Modernism" particularly is a misnomer, for we have had such teaching ever since men first doubted the supernatural revelation of God in His Book and in His Son.

God led me out of this bondage I mistook for liberty. My health became uncertain, and I returned to my old home in the hills. I spent many an hour in the woods back in my old haunts along the streams. Civic clubs of neighbouring towns began to invite me to deliver after-dinner speeches at various banquets and other gatherings. I prepared several collections of jokes with a moralising climax, and with these I fared forth now and then.

Father died in 1929, and mother and I were left in the old house, with only father's little grocery store to furnish a living. Some months later someone robbed the store and burned it to the ground. Surely the props were being knocked from under me, and I was awakened from my dreaming. The Lord was speaking to me, and gradually it was impressed on me that if I would return to the experience and the message of the "old-time religion," the Gospel I had preached as a boy, then the Lord would make a way for me.

I cannot say that there was any certain time when I made a sudden transition or a definite hour when all became bright as day. I did a lot of reading and praying. I remember that I read through J. Gresham Machen's *Christianity and Liberalism* at my hideout in the woods. As I now look over the record of my speaking engagements in those days I can see the change in the sermon titles and outlines. When such subjects as "The New Birth," "The Joy of Salvation," "Hell," and

"The Return of our Lord" begin to appear, it is not difficult to classify the preacher. I do know that the Lord brought me to a certainty and authority in believing and preaching His own Word instead of the surmisings of human wisdom.

With that there came an open door, a small door at first. For a while I was pastor of a little country church not far from my home. Then I was invited to Weeksville again, and for the fourth time I ministered there, for it was plainly the will of the Lord for me to give to these people who had borne with me through years of transition the definite message to which He had brought me.

I make no effort to analyse these years, to take them apart and put them back together. I know that many ministers are slipping to-day, and I question that argument is very effective with them. I am certain that no lecturing could have changed my notions about "the new freedom." I remember saying during that period that I could no more return to the old viewpoint than a chicken could return to its shell. The Lord must break us and remake us, but we can pray for all who are misled by "another Gospel" and win them if we may. I am certainly glad that I got out of the wilderness before these days of world distress set in.

I can testify that since I returned to the old message of "Ruin, Redemption, and Regeneration" the course of my life has been different. Mistakes have been made, of course, but the general movement has been forward and onward, and God has led and blessed in such a way as to leave no doubt of His guidance. More exciting than a story book has been the train of events since those days. Our God is a God of infinite variety and countless surprises, and nothing is so interesting and colourful as living in His will.

Many Christians are confused because while they may believe the Word of God and want to do the work of God they do not understand the will of God, particularly with regard to the times in which we live. Nothing has given me clearer perspective than the precious truth of Christ's return. During the idealistic days following World War I I shared the vision of world conversion and the brotherhood of man and universal peace through the gradual Christianization of humanity. I regarded the great prophetic portions of the Bible as apocalyptic puzzles. It makes a lot of difference what we believe about the future. If we don't know where we are going, we don't know what to do where we are. When it dawned on me that God is not converting the world but calling out a people for His Name, that threw a lot of light on all other matters as well. Blessed is the man who finds out which way God is moving and then gets going in the same direction!

VI

"BESIDE THE STILL WATERS"

I HAVE SPENT no happier days in all my life than my fourth stay in Weeksville, the three years of 1931-1934. The peaceful Carolina lowlands, the friendly farmer folk I had come to know so well, the long strolls along the country roads, the hours of meditation back on the creek at John Brown's farm, the happy Sundays at the church, the new joy of Bible study in my little room— all these things added up to a most satisfying and fruitful period of preparation for the work ahead.

The Bible study was something new, for, like many preachers, although I had read the Scriptures all my life, I had not really studied them seriously. I bought two Bibles and a large notebook, and pasting a column of Scripture down the center of each large page, I made notes on either side. In this way I went through the New Testament and some of the Old. On Wednesday evenings at prayer-meeting I followed a verse-by-verse study of the Word, a method also employed part of the time on Sunday mornings. There is no kind of preaching more rewarding to both preacher and people, but it means too much work for any disposed to get no further than employing a text as a convenient peg on which to hang a book review or a pulpit essay.

It does not take long to see the difference when the Word of God is preached and taught steadily week by week. I did not have to announce that I had another message than the philosophizing of my earlier ministry. Some whose consciences had been salved by my modernistic meanderings soon fell away, and others said, "This is a hard saying, who can hear it?" But the effect in other lives more than compensated. Several young people were led out into a definite call to Christian service and went away to prepare for it. The church paid out of debt, and when the Lord opened a new door, in Charleston, South Carolina, I left one of the most promising rural church opportunities I have ever known.

During this last stay at Weeksville I wrote my first book, *By The Still Waters*. Here again the Lord did for me what I had tried hard to do and failed. I had endeavoured to break into print for years, but except for the the newspaper work already referred to, a weekly column in the Charlotte, N.C., *Observer,* and some articles in church papers, I made little headway. I mailed my stuff and got it back accompanied by the familiar rejection slip until I lost heart. But when I began to "preach the preaching" God had bidden me, the way opened and I saw my first book published by the Fleming H. Revell Company of New York. *By The Still Waters* was a volume of rustic meditations, full of low-country atmosphere. It was a rare moment when the first shipment of my own books arrived. Although I have written nine more, *By The Still Waters* keeps well to the front in sales, and sometimes I wonder whether I have written anything better since!

Blessed is the man whom God has called to be a country preacher. Seldom does he know how favoured he is until he views that good estate in retrospect. Pity him if he uses his rural field for a springboard from which to leap into town. The country church is no mere proving ground for young preachers or dying ground for old ones. There is no more challenging opportunity on any boulevard. Country people are the backbone of the nation. Remove them and civilization would spoil overnight. They deserve the best in preachers. They have much to offer a minister. There he can be still amid the elemental simplicities of sun and sky and soil. He can garner many an illustration from growing things, as did his Master before him. He can minister to people who do not have the heebie-jeebies of city dwellers and who have time enough to make calm and steady appraisals. A devout rustic pastor is more capable of sober judgement than he likely will be later if he becomes a harried city preacher dashing from committee meeting to civic club to Ladies' Aid.

There is within every prophet the urge to rush to Carmel before he has tarried at Cherith. Alexander Whyte said Paul went to Arabia with Moses, the Psalms, and the Prophets in his knapsack and came back with Romans, Ephesians, and Colossians in his heart. I shall always thank God for the opportunity to learn something of what and why I believed out in the restful lowlands by the still waters.

43

Memory loves to dwell on those years. Sometimes I paddled a boat down Newbegun Creek. There was a "circuit" I loved to walk, several miles through rich farm lands, greeting now and then some of my people, stopping to see old Aunt Becky, who lived in a little cabin near the church. There were Negroes everywhere, and I picked up many a choice bit of their gentle wisdom, as when one of their philosophers once advised me, "Don't never squench the Spirit!" After all, "squench" being a combination of "squelch" and "quench," is a good word, even though it doesn't rate with Webster.

One incident lingers like a benediction. During my Weeksville years I kept hearing about a former pastor, one Josiah Elliott, who had shepherded the flock during the horse-and-buggy days. What a grip that man had on the hearts of those people. Even non-Christians would hold him up as an example of the kind of man they thought a Christian should be. "If we had more people like Josiah Elliott—" I heard again and again. I became very anxious to know something of the source of this man's power. Other preachers had followed him, men of greater scholarly and social attainments, but I heard most about Josiah Elliott. Finally, I went to my oracle, John Brown, back on the creek, and asked him where lay the secret springs of the old preacher's hold on the people, still strong after many years. I remember that John reflected for a moment as he was wont to do, and then remarked simply: "He just loved us."

I strolled back home along the pasture lane that afternoon, while from the cypress swamp near by the wood thrush chimed his vespers to the end of a perfect day. And in my heart there rang the old, old words we are so slow to learn: "Though I speak with the tongues of men and of angels and have not love, I am become as sounding brass, or a tinkling cymbal."

Josiah Elliott lived in the thirteenth chapter of First Corinthians. Would God it were the dwelling-place of us all!

VII

"AN OPEN DOOR"

"Delight thyself in the Lord and he shall give thee the desires of thine heart." How abundantly God has kept that promise in my own experience! I have already told how my desire to write was fulfilled only when I came into the will of the Lord. Along with my love for writing, my main interest through the years, as the reader has already observed, was a travelling ministry. From the boy-preacher days the life of an itinerant preacher was the chief desire of my heart. I think we sometimes have the impression that God's will is always something we do not like to do. The little boy who said, "This medicine must be good for me, it tastes so bad," was not unlike many Christians in their view of Providence. But His commandments are not grievous and while He may require us to do things which are not pleasant to our natural tastes. He is our Father, and we who believe are His children, and He delights to give us the desires of our hearts when our hearts are right.

But the Lord did not open the way until I began to preach the preaching He had bidden me. I tried to open doors that would not open, but I have learned since that when He opens a door no man can shut it. I could never do it in my own strength; it has been His own blessed work, and if He should withdraw His hand I would be as helpless as before. It has been a marvellous thing to watch the Lord go before and do so easily what I had struggled to accomplish, only to fail.

I had contributed some articles to *The Moody Monthly,* and to *Revelation,* then a new magazine, edited by Donald Grey Barnhouse of Philadelphia. One afternoon I was down at the Farmers Store, the general merchandise establishment in Weeksville, when a long-distance call from Philadelphia invited me to preach in the Tenth Presbyterian Church there. This was on a Thursday, and I was asked to preach on the Sunday following. I accepted and then almost wilted when I realised that I was going to preach where they had heard a lot of big preachers. The nearer I came to Philadelphia, the bigger it seemed. But I went, and the people were gracious, and I got along with two simple devotional messages. It was a considerable move from the quiet of my country pastorate, but it encouraged my heart and brought me into a circle of friends whose fellowship I have prized through the years.

Next, I was invited to speak at Columbia Bible College in Columbia, South Carolina, and to address a fellowship of Christians in Augusta, Georgia, a group that had been led to Christ by the Bible teaching of Mrs. T. C. Rounds. Something of the ministry of Mrs. Rounds has been related by my friend Richard Ellsworth Day in his remarkable biography of Henry Parsons Crowell, *Breakfast Table Autocrat.* Later I spent two weeks at Camp Tappuah near Asheville, North Carolina, a camp of fine young people under the direction of the Hampden-DuBose Academy. I shall never forget the impression these consecrated young people made on me. I was there to minister to them, but they also ministered to me. I had not known of the many groups of Christians all over the country turning back to the Bible and the old message, the many centers of fundamental preaching and teaching where believers of all denominations are feeding their souls on the Word of God. Thousands of church members today do not know that there are two movements in the church today. One is known as fundamentalism the other as modernism, the issue between them being whether we have a truly inspired record in the Bible and a Christ who was all He claimed to be and did all He is reported to have done, or a Bible that contains here and there—depending on where you want to locate it—the Word of God, and a patched-up Christ pieced together by sorting out the false and true accounts, a hopeless procedure, since no two investigators ever end with the same pieces.

But, deplorable as the modern apostasy may be, the Bible believer need not take to the juniper tree. There are vastly more than the Biblical "seven thousand who have not bowed to Baal." Among these are staunch and steady men in major denominations who stay in their pulpits and preach the Word. Others have felt led to come out and be independent. There are radio preachers and Bible schools and Bible conferences and taberna-

48

cles. Of course, there have been some who have gone about a good thing in a bad way. There is some extremism and much contention and energy of the flesh and sins of the spirit. Nevertheless, in spite of all hindrances, God's Spirit is moving and there is a sound of a going in the mulberry trees. To try to organise it is dangerous, because the breath of the Spirit does not yield to a lot of American high-pressure promotion. A lot of energy now being burned up trying to put it over might better be used listening to God, getting in line with His will, and obeying Him in godly living. The Early Church, on fire for God, got along amazingly well with a minimum of program, propaganda, and paraphernalia. It moved the world by the Spirit, and slowed down only when it tried to make itself perfect in the flesh.

Now and then there is a resurgence of New Testament Christianity, which always starts with simple, Spirit-filled witnessing to Jesus Christ. Then it moves along mightily, until it bogs up in machinery designed to speed its progress. Finally, the Spirit abandons the wreck and starts somewhere else anew. It was with such a present-day movement of the Spirit that I became acquainted and identified during my last stay at Weeksville. It is a precious fellowship of those who fear the Lord and speak often one to another. It is a delightful experience to discover that, no matter where we go, there are always some who gather to hear about the Book, the Blood, and the Blessed Hope. It is a mighty movement, and it would be amusing if it were not so pathetic how ignorant of this work of God many experts at studying trends and analysing the times seem to be. If they really do not know, one wonders where they have been, for this thing is not being done in a corner. If it is wilful ignorance, that is infinitely worse.

This modern stirring of the Spirit speaks around the world in such radio preachers as Charles E. Fuller and Walter Maier. It has dotted the land with Bible schools in the wake of the apostasy of so many colleges and seminaries. It has gathered Christians into Bible conferences and restored the Word of God to its place of authority. It has packed thousands of youth into rallies on the devil's Saturday night. Believers in the old-time religion need not fret over those moderns who like to think we are extinct. Somewhat like Paul to the Philippian jailer, we would say to all such in this present-day crisis, "Do thyself no harm, we are still here."

VIII

"IF ANY MAN THIRST . . ."

CHARLESTON, SOUTH CAROLINA, is the capital of that historic low country, which Archibald Rutledge has described with such quiet charm. Its First Baptist Church, organised in 1683, is the oldest Baptist church in the South. The quaint, solid church building on Church Street is an attraction in itself. The high-ceilinged auditorium, the gallery where formerly sat the slaves, the great windows and box pews with doors and footrests, all are saturated with the spirit of the Old South, the atmosphere of another day before the modern whirl we misnamed progress came along. While I was pastor, there was presented to the church the pulpit Bible used by the Revolutionary War pastor—and the church was quite old then! The building is the third used by the church but the organization goes back to the days of George Whitfield who preached in Charleston on his American tours.

The old church had seen better days than when I first saw it in 1934. Only a handful of the faithful still carried on, but among them were some dear souls who truly loved the Lord. They had steadily opposed the closing or absorption of the church, and believed God still had a mission for it to fulfil. There was nothing about it to attract a preacher looking for something easy. It presented innumerable difficulties, and a brother remarked that it was a "has-been," but I felt that it was also a "can-be" by God's grace, and so began five years with the "old city by the sea."

What followed was a ministry intensive rather than extensive. The Lord was pleased to quicken the spiritual life of many of the people, and we witnessed some precious experiences, of both conversion and consecration. In my travels since I left Charleston I have found many of my former flock who have moved here and there and continued to testify to the blessing of those days we spent together. The mid-week prayer meeting and a young people's devotional gathering on Friday nights especially delighted our souls and left enduring memories. The Sunday attendance was never large, and the increase in membership, while substantial, was not impressive, but a trail was blazed and a foundation laid in a prophetic rather than pastoral ministry. A weekly radio broadcast gave us the ear of the town and community, and extra appointments at other churches, a baccalaureate sermon at the Citadel, well-known military college of the city; outdoor meetings in Hampton Park, and other outside services gave wider range to our message.

It was during my early days in Charleston that I became acquainted with a dear saint of God known as Granny Russell. She was very old and her eyesight was failing but she was an exuberant Christian. On one of my visits, as I started to leave, she put a hand on my shoulder and said, "Just in case you need a deeper touch on your ministry, I'll pray about it." Then she gave me a copy of *Deeper Experiences of Famous Christians*. That night in my room I couldn't sleep until I had read the book, and then I couldn't sleep because I had read it! It created in my heart a thirst to be filled with the Spirit. Many an evening was spent down in the old church, meditating and praying, and many afternoons I walked the beach out on the Isle of Palms, a good place to pray aloud by the roaring surf. I thank God for those days. I was convinced that there was for me "something better." Faith had caught the joyful sound, the song of saints on higher ground. The Lord brought me to see the need not only of knowing Christ and having a message to preach but also of an enduement of the Spirit for power in life and testimony. Some are so afraid of "getting out on a limb" on this subject that they never even get up the tree! They are like beggars discussing the relative merits of different kinds of pock-etbooks—and all of them "broke." Some would rather miss a blessing than give up a prejudice. Whatever we may call it—filling of the Spirit, enduement, victorious life, perfect love—too many Christians know nothing of it. And many an Apollos has to learn from Aquila and Priscilla, maybe in his own congregation, as did Moody in his day, the secret of living not by human reserves but by heavenly resources.

At length, I came to the blessed truth of John 7:37-39: "If any man thirst, let him come unto me and drink. He that believeth on me, as the scripture hath said, from within him shall flow rivers of living water. But this spake he of the Spirit which they that believe on him should receive: for the Holy Ghost was not yet given; because that Jesus was not yet glorified." I saw that it was a matter of thirsting, coming, drinking, believing, overflowing. There was no great emotional experience, but just as I had trusted Christ as my Saviour, so by simple faith I received the filling of the Spirit, who had already regenerated me and who dwelt within.

It has been said that the two words "believe" and "receive" are the hardest for most people to spell correctly, because it is "ie" in one and "ei" in the other. Surely, in Christian experience they are slowly learned by so many of us, and yet they are the key words in the language of things spiritual. To as many as RECEIVE Him our Lord gives the right to become the sons of God, even to them that BELIEVE on His Name. What things soever we desire when we pray, we are to BELIEVE that we RECEIVE them, and we shall have them. And Jesus spoke of the Spirit which they that BELIEVE on Him should RECEIVE. Paul Rader's song uses the key words:

> "Speak, Lord; before Thy throne we wait,
>   Thy promise we BELIEVE;
>   And will not let Thee go until
>   The blessing we RECEIVE."

There is indeed much counterfeit teaching and experience along this line to-day, but it is only the devil's device to scare us away from the genuine. Some are not filled because they must first be emptied. Even God cannot fill what is already full. To be filled with the Spirit is every Christian's duty, because the Word commands it. It is not the privilege of a favored few. The purpose of it is that we may exalt Christ and not boast of some strange experience. If we thirst and come to Christ in full surrender, we have a right to drink. If it takes time, it is not that God is reluctant but that we are rebellious and must get quiet and receptive before Him. There is nothing hit-or-miss about it. True, the wind bloweth where it listeth, and the wind and the Spirit operate in similar ways, but the wind obeys law, and the laws of spiritual power are just as fixed and definite. Campbell Morgan said, "Obey the law of the wind and the wind will obey you." Surely, if scientists can give themselves without stint these days to pondering and proving atomic power, the saints of God ought to make it their business to demonstrate apostolic power. God has challenged us to prove Him, and His eyes run to and fro throughout the whole earth, waiting to shew Himself strong in the behalf of them whose heart is perfect toward Him. God is sovereign, and His Spirit manifests Himself in different ways, sometimes spectacularly, and maybe secretly and silently; but there is for us abundant power to do what God wants done.

While I was in Charleston, calls for Bible conferences and church meetings continued to come. A two-week's engagement with the First Baptist Church of Minneapolis, Minnesota, where for forty years Dr. W. B. Riley championed the truth, opened new doors in the Middle West. Dr. Riley proved himself to be a great and helpful friend. Moody Bible Institute invited me to its annual Youth Rally, where on Labor Day for four consecutive years I ministered in the old auditorium to fine gatherings of young people. The Moody Conference in Philadelphia, the Prophetic Conference in New York, Medicine Lake and Cedar Lake summer conferences were delightful experiences during this period. It was evident that the Lord was opening a travelling ministry. So I left Charleston in 1939, after five years there, and went first to my old home in the hills for a month, to spend the last Christmas I was to enjoy with my mother. Nothing is more helpful to one launching out in a new venture than to get back in more ways than one to the source from which he started, to renew the covenant, and to lay hold of fresh grace for days ahead. So I began a new "journey from Jugtown."

IX

"I HAD FAINTED UNLESS . . ."

No JOURNEY IS COMPLETE that does not lead through some dark valleys. We can properly comfort others only with the comfort wherewith we ourselves have been comforted of God. No single experience of mine has been more rewarding in lessons learned and passed on to others than a two-year round of nervous exhaustion and depression with subsequent deliverance.

There are two kinds of people: nervous people and people who laugh at nervous people. For years I was one of the latter, regarding the "imaginary" sufferings of others with little sympathy. I had very fine theories on the subject, much like a bachelor on how to rear a family. But once I was afflicted, all my prescriptions were like the usual round of rheumatism cures.

I had been going hard, with a mind divided between a pastorate and a travelling ministry. One night in a farm home in Iowa I went to bed as usual but discovered that I could not sleep. Next night I repeated the performance. From then on for many months the sleep I had always taken for granted became very precious because very scarce. I suppose I slept more than I thought, else I would have died or lost my mind; but I seemed to sleep almost not at all. How little do we value life's dearest possessions while we have them! Everybody accepts sleep as a matter of course. One just goes to sleep and that is all there is to it. But to-day, when the use of sleeping pills and powders is at an all-time high, many are learning that our commonest blessings are often hardest to regain when lost.

Along with my sleeplessness came depression. Only the "initiated" can understand the nameless fears, the ghosts and goblins that look into the windows of minds so distressed. They may be imaginary and we may laugh at them later, but they are real enough while they last. One is reminded of the coloured man who discovered one night that he was in a graveyard. Making a headlong exit, he fell over tombstones and scratched himself badly among the briars and bushes. Next day someone asked, "Don't you know ghosts can't hurt you?" "I knows dat," replied the victim, "but dey can make you hurt yo'sel'." The apparitions that haunt the dismal days of exhausted souls and play such sinister tunes on worn-out nerves can cause plenty of trouble. No point is gained in merely making light of the matter.

I did not quit preaching, although sometimes I had to hold to the pulpit to steady myself. At first I was alarmed and panicky, but I began to study the subject and found that many of the Lord's servants, including some truly great souls, had been through the same deep waters. It comforted me no little to learn that Spurgeon had been much beset in his day by depression. No wonder he found such solace in the Psalms, where, to use his own words, "David chideth David out of the dumps." Isaac Watts was an insomniac for years, and his line about "the Comfort of my nights" was more than poetry. I read the experiences of Dr. Torrey and James McConkey and many others. And I did not forget that the two most rugged characters in the Bible, Elijah in the Old Testament, and the New Testament Elijah, John the Baptist, had something akin to nervous breakdowns. The Lord dealt gently with them both, for He knoweth our frame and remembereth that we are dust. Perhaps a Christian is never nearer to the Lord and never feels farther from Him than when passing in this fashion through a Slough of Despond.

If ever I walked by "dry faith" it was during those days. I remember a little motto on the wall of my room that read, "Why Art Thou Disquieted? . . . Hold Fast Your Confidence." I preached when I could not feel anything I preached. There were times when I could not pray. Satan assailed me with doubts about my salvation. Dr. Ironside's book, *Full Assurance,* was a great help. Likewise a story Dr. Richard Ellsworth Day told me in his California home—he has put it in print—*Let 'Er Rip!*

There was no sudden deliverance. I learned to rest more. I came to the conclusion that God is not interested in mere quantity production and that we sometimes can do more by doing less. I have listened to some husky go-getters speak slightingly of those who cannot stand their pace, but I have learned to pay no attention to them. Every man must be fully persuaded in his own mind and work out a system in line with his own make-up and limitations. I have watched some start out in a fury to end in a flop, go up like a rocket and come down like a rock. Others become so ragged-edged that their irritable dispositions cancel a lot of the good they endeavour to do. Our Lord asked, "Are there not twelve hours in the day?" There is always time enough to do God's will; what takes so much time is doing what we want to do. "He that believeth shall not make haste." I have no sympathy with those who say the devil never takes a vacation. I am not following the devil but the Lord, who said, "Come ye yourselves apart . . . and rest awhile."

Along with learning some common sense rules, I was helped most, so far as human assistance is concerned, by the good wife the Lord gave me. Of that I shall speak more fully in the next chapter. She had been through the same sort of experience and understood. Says Alexander Whyte: "For in how many sloughs do men lie till this daughter of Help give them her hand, and out of how many more sloughs are they all their days by her delivered and kept!"

After I was delivered, I put something of what I had gathered into the little book, *Rest Awhile*. A Youth for Christ leader told me how one night alone in a cabin where he had gone to rest and to stave off a collapse his hand fell upon *Rest Awhile* and a certain chapter gave him needed help when he was unable to sleep. A distressed mother picked up a copy from some books her daughter had brought home. She found something she needed in it. A young preacher and his wife told me that they were going through severe testing when a message in the little book gave much assistance. So there was a purpose in those doleful years, and I speak of them here only to encourage someone similarly tried.

X

"WHOSO FINDETH A WIFE . . ."

AFTER A MONTH in the country following my departure
from Charleston, I launched out to begin, with the
opening of 1940, a full-time travelling ministry. But
immediately I ran into a severe testing. I had been invited by Mel Trotter to speak in his Grand Rapids
Mission in early January. I got as far as Chicago, where,
after a week of broadcasting from Moody Bible Institute, I came down with flu, spent a week in a hospital,
and was forced to cancel a string of appointments. I
shall never forget those weeks. The devil, the accuser,
camped on the foot of my bed, saying: "You should
never have gone into this work, and this is what you
get for trying it."

It was a dreadfully cold winter, and when I had begun to recover, the doctor ordered me to head South if
I could. I went straight to Tampa, Florida, where I
recuperated and soon was able to take meetings. Two
delightful weeks were spent at the Hampton-DuBose
Academy in Orlando, preaching in the First Presbyterian Church along with Dr. Bob Jones, Sr., Dr. Charles
G. Trumbull, Miss Ruth Paxson, and Dr. R. E. Neighbour.

But God had something still better for me. Out where

I was resting there was a gracious little lady whom I had met on a previous visit. We had not particularly impressed each other before, but this time she had mercy on this lonely sick preacher, prepared suitable food for him, and played dominoes with him before the big open fire. The food did its part on the old road to a man's heart, but more than food I needed fellowship and companionship, and so the long strolls in Florida sunshine by day and Florida moonlight by night convinced me that Providence in routing me out of Chicago had known better than I what I needed. I was puzzled for the moment, because one reason for entering the travelling ministry had been that I was unattached and had no home. But love prevailed, and when I left Florida to start out again on my interrupted circuit, the love and letters of Sara Allred gave a new light and colour to my venture. Sara had grown up in a lovely Quaker home in Greensboro, North Carolina, not very far from my own home, but we had never heard of each other until we met in Florida. From the very first dinner we had together, as guests of Homer Rodeheaver, we have enjoyed an ever-widening circle of friends who have rejoiced with us in our happiness.

In late March of 1940 I resumed the trail again, speaking with the Moody Conference in Park Street Church in Boston and taking Monday evenings in Calvary Baptist Church in New York for a month. There followed a week with Bob Jones College, a commencement address for the Philadelphia School of the Bible in the Baptist Temple, and a Sunday with the First Baptist

Church of New York. Summer conferences included Hawthorne and Keswick, New Jersey, and Saginaw Bay and Maranatha in Michigan. Meetings in Lynchburg, Virginia, Providence, Rhode Island, and Newport News, Virginia, with another Youth Rally at Moody Bible Institute, completed a busy summer and fall. I enjoyed a few days back at Weeksville again, meeting old friends and preaching twice in my old church.

It was during that summer that mother passed away. I was called home from Maranatha Conference in Michigan, and I remember Dr. Bob Jones, Sr., putting his arm around my neck and having a word of prayer with me before I started. Mother's last word to me she had dictated to my brother only a few days before, as they prepared a letter between them. "Tell Vance to keep up the good fight," she had said, "for God is with him, and 'if God be for us, who can be against us?'"

I returned to the old home in October, bought the little farm, and spent the month writing my book, *Rest Awhile.* It was the sixth in a series I had found time to prepare, *By The Still Waters, Secret of Christian Joy, Consider Him, Blood, Bread and Fire* and *Road To Revival* having preceded it. I had peculiar joy in writing *Rest Awhile,* for the Lord had given me such a blessed year that I could rest with real satisfaction. Whatever fears I had suffered at the outset of my travelling ministry were now dissolved: the Lord had set His seal upon it and I took fresh courage while I rested on the old front porch at cotton-picking time.

After another preaching circuit, I ended the year's

work with two messages in the Fourth Presbyterian Church in Washington. On Saturday morning, December 14, I was married to the gracious little lady whose love and prayers and letters had helped so much to make 1940 the happy year it was. There was a very simple ceremony in her home at nine o'clock, and we left at ten for California. Doors had opened on the West Coast, and while we hesitated at first to undertake such a heavy schedule for our first joint venture, we felt that the Lord was in it, and so it gloriously proved to be. The winter was spent in meetings up and down the Coast, closing in Los Angeles in the Church of the Open Door. Then we returned East, stopping off at Salt Lake City for two meetings, and finishing with two weeks in Mid-West Bible Church in Chicago, where Torrey Johnson was the very able pastor.

"Whoso findeth a wife findeth a good thing and obtained a favour of the Lord." I can heartily say "Amen" to the words of Solomon: "Two are better than one; because they have a good reward for their labour. For if they fall, the one will lift up his fellow: but woe to him that is alone when he falleth; for he hath not another to help him up." Whitefield wrote, "My wife and I go on like two happy pilgrims, leaning on our Beloved." I have at least that much in common with Whitefield. It took almost forty years for me to find a wife, but then the Israelites were forty years in the wilderness! Some seem to enjoy making embarrassing wisecracks about their wives. I have never seen the point. I would never think of making such remarks about my mother, then why should I so speak of my wife? Some poor mortals may have been married under orange blossoms and found they had a lemon just the same, but they should not bore the rest of us because of their misfortune.

Those who acknowledge the Lord in this matter find that, as in all other matters, He directs our paths. One day a coloured elevator girl said to me, "You and your wife seem so happy—are you a minister?" Even the world connects a happy married life with the things of God. It need never be otherwise for those who marry "in the Lord."

XI

"IN JOURNEYINGS OFTEN . . ."

THE ITINERANT MINISTRY, which began full-time in 1940, has carried this scribe all over the United States, preaching in churches of many denominations, in tabernacles, tents, schools, public auditoriums, and over the radio. A cross section of conservative, evangelical Christianity has been visited. Memory now recounts many interesting experiences.

Moody Bible Institute's great annual event, Founder's Week, attracts the faithful from far and near, speakers from home and abroad. One night in Moody Memorial Church I shall never forget. I was the second speaker on a double-header featuring, first, the Chief Chaplain of the Navy. When he finished, the hour was late and the great congregation, packing all available space was unpredictable. Would they listen to another message? I breathed a prayer and started my sermon, and the Lord came to this poor preacher's relief and granted a liberty and response I shall long remember.

Two weeks in People's Church, Toronto, well known among evangelicals by reason of the ministry of Oswald J. Smith, also comes to mind. A constant evangelistic campaign goes on there, with a pageant of preachers through the year. Dr. Smith has covered much territory in his wide ministry by pen and tongue, and his messages breathe the old-time revival atmosphere.

Calvary Baptist Church, New York, is another Gospel beehive. Several conferences there have gained us a circle of friends in the metropolis. It has been our privilege to minister in the Gospel Tabernacle where A. B. Simpson laboured for many years, and in the First Baptist Church, where Dr. I. M. Haldeman stood so long as a prophet of God.

The Church of the Open Door, Los Angeles, is a perennial center of evangelism and Bible-teaching. Here Dr. Torrey and many another pulpit giant have ministered in days gone by. In Atlanta, Georgia, the Baptist Tabernacle, begun under the Spirit-filled leadership of Len G. Broughton, carries on conferences similar to those of his day. Park Street Church in Boston is another landmark that stands like a lighthouse and sounds forth no uncertain message.

Summers have been spent in the Bible conferences which God has raised up all over America, successors to the old-time camp meetings. Winona Lake is perhaps the largest, with its many meetings going on most of the day. I see more preachers from everywhere there and at Founder's Week in Chicago than anywhere else. I always enjoy a meal or two at Homer Rodeheaver's "Rainbow Point," where the rainbow motif shows up even on the table napkins and the genial spirit of Rody pervades the scene. Mrs. Billy Sunday has also shown us many interesting mementoes of the great days of her famous husband. To look over the autographed pictures

of America's great and to read the volumes of newspaper clippings from a day when evangelism made
front-page headlines in great dailies is enough to prove
that a lot of water has run under the bridge since then.

Over our land each summer the conferences lure
lovers of the Word, and what a joy it has been to minister in many of them: Montrose, where Dr. Torrey lies
buried; Keswick, New Jersey, with its deep note of victorious living; Medicine Lake, Minnesota, a grand spot
with a splendid set-up; Maranatha, Michigan, a growing
gathering place where Dr. H. H. Savage and Howard
Skinner team up to do a fine job; the Firs at Belling-
ham, Washington, with its atmosphere of reverence and
devotion; Mt. Hermon in California, among the big
trees, a constant surge of Christian activity all summer;
Ben Lippen, near my own home in North Carolina,
truly a "mountain of trust"; Pinebrook, Pennsylvania,
the only one of its kind, where Percy Crawford carries
on a great work in his own remarkable way. Pinebrook
would wreck some super-dignified Pharisees in one day,
but an understanding heart can soon see the point in
this Pocono power-dam.

Another type of conference I discovered in the New
England Fellowship circuit while travelling over the
six states for weeks, preaching a night in a place. Many
were small churches and congregations were not usually
large; the schedule was strenuous, but there was rich
reward in meeting many earnest Christians and faithful
pastors holding fast and holding forth.

The Youth for Christ movement is a phenomenon

that has swept the land. I knew many of the leaders even in earlier days, and have counted it a privilege to work with Jack Wyrtzen, Torrey Johnson, Bob Cook, Richard Harvey, Roger Malsbary, George Wilson, and many others. Youth for Christ has occupied many a Saturday night I used to give to resting, but there have been many fine compensations.

So this ministry has gone on, reaching into churches of many persuasions: Baptist, Methodist, Presbyterian, Reformed, Brethren, Mennonite, Christian and Missionary Alliance, and independent branches. I have enjoyed liberty in preaching wherever God opened the door. I have always felt that any man with God's message need not cool his heels in anybody's office, waiting to ask if he might preach in somebody's church. There is blessed freedom in being under no orders from any headquarters except from God above. When the disciples returned from their early preaching trips, they reported to Christ, not to a committee. I have avoided entangling alliances and joined no groups and espoused no movements, feeling that by being free from them I can best serve them.

There are enough movements and counter-movements to-day to keep an observer busier than a one-eyed man at a three-ring circus. God often raises up the irregular when the regular fails to function, but He uses the irregular only to open up the regular channels again: they serve God only as they serve His church. I believe in the Church and in loyalty to a local church. I am not in favour of that view of the invisible church that makes one invisible at church on Sunday morning. Christ left a church, and all religious movements have value only as they are handmaidens to the Church. If the churches were Spirit-filled and about their real business, we would need none of the extra organizations which have sprung up because of the failure of churches to meet the situation. I work with both, but I consider the ideal to be a New Testament local church on fire for God, teaching the believers and winning the lost, sufficient through the Spirit for all its opportunities and efficient in all its work.

XII

"THE BATTLE IS THE LORD'S"

THE RECITAL of one's experiences in the travelling ministry soon grows monotonous to the reader. But the fellowship with earnest Christians all over the land, the joy of seeing men and women move out into full consecration, the supreme delight of witnessing conversions, these linger with the preacher, and a wealth of blessed memories gathers with the years. To learn that someone took a stand for Christ years ago in a meeting somewhere and now is faithfully serving the Lord, to discover that when you preached a sermon that seemed a failure God used it to transform a life, this is the richest compensation of a travelling preacher. Letters revealing that hearts have been blessed by a sermon or book are the best pay checks one can ever receive.

An Army chaplain asked me one morning in Moody Church, "Do you remember preaching in Waterloo, Iowa, several years ago, when only one man stood on your invitation? I am that man." In Bethany Reformed Church, Chicago, a member of the Wheaton Glee Club asked me, "Do you remember preaching in Detroit Lakes, Minnesota, when only one girl came forward?" (I certainly could remember it, for I thought the meeting was a failure.) "Well, I am that girl, and

I am now ready to go to Africa as a missionary as soon as I can get passage."

How often does God turn what seemed a failure into a triumph! It is best to let Him keep the books and make no final appraisal of any effort in His Name, judging nothing before the time. I remember speaking at a youth gathering when my subject was Baruch. Most of them had never heard of that minor Old Testament character. I prepared a rather heavy sermon that was, it seemed to me, as complete a dud as I ever inflicted on the public. I resolved to give Baruch a long rest so far as my interest in him was concerned—a foolish procedure, since it wasn't his fault. But some years later, a young lady told me that the message on Baruch was a turning point in her life. It is not possible to gauge fairly any service or sermon, since so much is always hidden from our eyes.

I treasure a sheaf of letters from old and young, some from foreign lands, testifying to blessings received from sermon or book or magazine article. The usual percentage of crackpots, of course, make their contribution, and queer tracts, strange poems, and weird communications are chaff mixed with the wheat. But most of the writers belong to the "seven thousand who have not bowed to Baal," who fear the Lord and speak often one to another. What a precious fellowship it is, and well may we exhort one another and so much the more as we see the Day approaching.

Plenty of advice is offered, and a minister must boil it down and take what he can use. I remember that, after I had preached rather severely on one occasion, a brother handed me a tract on love, which he evidently thought I needed. I took it to heart and next evening gave a rather subdued message. That night another dear brother said to me, "It'll take hell-fire preaching to wake up this crowd!" I thought of the man who tried to live by proverbs but ran into trouble trying to balance "Look before you leap" with "He who hesitates is lost."

I received a letter sternly censuring me for too much humour in a certain address. Someone had listened over the radio and was shocked to hear so much laughing in a religious service. What she did not know was that in that same meeting one minister came to a crisis and a spiritual victory.

I have never been able to designate exactly the nature of my work. I am not a professional evangelist or a Bible teacher. I often tell people that I am just a Baptist preacher doing a little Methodist exhorting. I have majored in application rather than interpretation. Sam Jones used to say that mustard in a can on the shelf would do no good but that it must be put into a poultice and applied. So the Word must be laid close to the trouble. I have felt that there is great need to-day for the New Testament prophet who speaks to edification, exhortation, and comfort, a strengthening, stirring and soothing ministry. In my own work I have endeavoured to balance the revivalistic note with the devotional, even in my books alternating a book of sermons with a volume of meditations. It helps the writer and provides the reader, I trust, with a more balanced fare.

Some time ago a brother asked, "How does one get into Bible conference work?" He spoke as though there were some wire-pulling technique whereby one "gets to know the right people" and so promotes himself. I know of no such procedure so far as my own ministry is concerned. One day, while rummaging through some old diaries at home, I came across this entry: "Approaching thirty. One little rural church. I sit on a rainy afternoon waiting to go there and preach." I can account for the busy years since only by saying, "It is the Lord." No planning or striving of my own could have opened the doors. I tried that when I was out of God's will. With a batch of posters, I tried to speak in court-houses and schools. Once I had a crowd when the fire alarm was rung by mistake and a throng gathered, not for my lecture but for the fire. When the Lord Himself opens the door no man can shut it. And there is added liberty in knowing that He has cleared the way. I have no ability whatever for promoting anything, and if the Lord should cease to send in the calls my work would fold up overnight, for I am under no auspices and am backed by no board or agency.

My wife and I have seen Pullman space and hotel rooms open up during the war years when they just "weren't to be had." Not once did I sit up all night for lack of a berth. Through all the crowded wartime conditions we learned that God is greater than all human emergencies and will put His workers where He wants them. Humanly, I have found myself bewildered and fearful more than once, only to learn that God is more than able to meet the "ifs" and "buts" of circumstance. Some try to bulldoze their way through by being "tough," but far better it is to remember that "the battle is the Lord's," to stand still and see Him work it out.

One illustration of this blessed truth stands out. I had finished a meeting in Baltimore on a Sunday night and was due to being in La Salle, Illinois, on the Monday night following. Some said it couldn't be done with wartime train schedules. I was due to arrive in La Salle at seven and preach at seven-thirty. Next morning I noticed that the Pullman seat opposite mine was occupied by a prominent government official. He was on his way to speak in Chicago. Some pressure was brought to bear on his behalf and we really went through on time. I sat and looked at him—a cat may look at a king—and thought, "You may think you are getting through on time because you are to speak in Chicago, but the good Lord is just getting this little preacher through on time to speak in La Salle!" I had the government working for me! So, while it may seem that man's plans are being given the main line to-day, unknown to this world, God is seeing His own program through. The smallest Christian, if he be in line with God's great purpose, can see his Father making even the wrath of men to praise Him and working out, amid all the clamour of this age, His own eternal will.

If we are listening to the still, small voice we shall not

go wrong. Some time ago, while seeking to ascertain the leading of the Lord as to the messages I was to give at Founder's Week Conference in Chicago, I felt impressed to prepare three sermons. But I was scheduled to speak only twice and could not understand the reason for the extra sermon. I spent some time trying to decide which of the three not to use. But it turned out that the scheduled speaker for the final afternoon, Premier Manning of Alberta, did not arrive on time and I had to pinch-hit for him. So I used my three sermons after all. I might have spared myself all that bother, for our Father knows what He is doing. "The battle is the Lord's."

XIII

"TO BE A CHRISTIAN"

I HAVE RELATED how I began my ministry preaching the simple Gospel message generally preached during my boyhood days. It was good Gospel and still is. Most of those earlier preachers were not dispensationalists. They believed, for instance, in one general judgement. I have changed my mind about that but I wish that many who now believe in several judgements could preach them with the fervour those old-timers had when they held forth on "Prepare To Meet Thy God." We sang "There's A Great Day Coming" and "We Are Passing Away To That Great Judgement Day." We lumped the events into one Great Assize, but there was a profound and overwhelming seriousness about it that sadly needs to be recovered to-day.

I have related also how, for a while, I was enamoured of the modern approach and then was delivered. My first reaction was to be a rather belligerent fundamentalist, calling down fire on all the Samaritans who did not dot all their *i's* and cross all their *t's* as I did. Someone asked an Irishman: "If you and the English could settle all your difficulties, what would you Irishmen do?" He replied, "I'm sure the Lord would provide: He would never leave an Irishman without grounds for a fight." There was something of that in my fundamentalism.

Eventually, I came to the conclusion which I have been preaching ever since: the issue is simply Jesus Christ. By Him all things consist. The issue is not your little crowd or mine. When the disciples would have Jesus reprove others who were casting out demons, He made Himself the issue: "He that is not against us is on our part." Again, He said, "He that is not with me is against me; and he that gathereth not with me scattereth abroad." The issue is not, Are they with your outfit? but Are they with Christ? To his own Master every man standeth or falleth.

Christ is the issue. He is the issue in salvation, for there is none other name under heaven given among men whereby we must be saved. He is the issue in consecration and separation. "Let us go forth therefore unto him without the camp, bearing his reproach." It is a person-to-Person affair.

> "My Jesus, I love Thee,
>   I know Thou art mine;
>   For Thee all the follies of sin I resign."

Look at the pronouns in that verse. It is a personal matter between the believer and His Lord.

Christ is the Deeper Life, or whatever you like to call it. "To me to live is CHRIST." He is the issue in doctrine. "I am the resurrection and the life." The resurrection is a Person. We need to move back from the doctrinal to the personal, for all doctrine consists by

Him. He is the hub, and we need not perch on our favourite spokes like owls on limbs. We can stand at the Hub, and then all the spokes are ours. And the closer we are to the Hub, the closer we are to all the spokes. When we make anything less than Christ Himself the issue we are making the part greater than the whole.

If Christ is the issue there is a corollary: for us the issue is just to be Christians. "The disciples were called Christians first at Antioch." They have been called many things since, but they never had a better name. No sect has a monopoly on that. The issue is not fundamentalism. That name has been bandied about so much that it has come to mean anything from a brand of Mormons in Utah to snake-handlers in West Virginia and Jehovah's Witnesses everywhere. When J. Gresham Machen titled his book *Christianity and Liberalism* he was wise. What we call fundamentalism, true fundamentalism, is simply old-fashioned New Testament Christianity. We do not need a new name. We have a name, we are just Christians. Let the modernists get a new name. They need one, for there is nothing modern about modernism, nothing liberal about liberalism.

Why not just be Christians? I am not discounting loyalty to church or denomination. A man is a better citizen of America if he is loyal to his own family and town. But often we are devoted to a church or organization, in love with our fundamentalism, loyal to men and movements but not to Christ. Like Ephesus, we have left our first love. First of all, let us be Christians. The situation is too serious, the need too urgent, and the time too short for anything else. A lot of our religious programs to-day are beside the point. It is too late in the day for them. They are trying to meet a short-term emergency with a long-range plan.

Is it going to take the fires of persecution, holy desperation, to make us gather around Christ? The only place where you will ever get the Christians together is where they are already together, in Him. Babel was man's plan of unity and God cursed it with tongues no one could understand. Pentecost was God's plan of unity and He blessed it with tongues everyone could understand. We are not calling for unanimity, we will never have that. We are not asking for unification, that is man-made. We pray for unity, and we have that in Christ.

A church had a sign in front: "JESUS ONLY." One night a storm blew out the first three letters and left "US ONLY." Too many churches have come to that.

The issue is Christ. Not the Christ of modernism— that is a false Christ. Not the Christ of partyism, "I of Christ." Simply Jesus Christ Himself, Son of God, virgin-born, who lived a sinless life, died a substitutionary, atoning death, rose bodily from the grave, is coming again. To know Him and to make Him known, that is enough. The New Testament speaks of being called Christians—there is our name. It speaks of suffering as a Christian—it costs. It tells us that Paul sought to persuade Agrippa to be a Christian. Paul was a persuader because he was persuaded—persuaded that Christ was able to keep, persuaded that nothing could separate him from God's love. And, knowing the terror of the Lord, he persuaded men. Every Christian should be a persuader.

What is a New Testament Christian? Simply a believer on the Lord Jesus Christ, Spirit-filled and witnessing. Before Agrippa, Paul told his experience, showing himself to be a believer. Then "having therefore obtained help of God"—he was Spirit-filled—"I continue witnessing." And what was his message? "None other things than those which the prophets and Moses did say should come"—that is the Old Testament—"that Christ should suffer and that He should be the first that should rise from the dead"—that is the Gospel.

A believer, Spirit-filled, witnessing. Why can't we just be Christians? I am going up and down the country endeavouring to call men back to the Center. We get lost out on the circumference. I am not organising anything. I have no blanks to sign, no buttons to wear. I am not trying to start a new movement. We have so many movements now that we can't move! I am not trying to be a leader. We are over-supplied with brass hats already. Some little boys were playing war. When an onlooker asked why they were so quiet, one boy replied, "We're all generals, we can't get anybody to do the fighting!"

I am weary of all our plans and projects that waste time, energy, and money in duplicating each other. If we spent the time in prayer that we use trying to outdo each other, we would have a revival now.

The issue is Christ. We assume that we already know that, but we assume it when we ought to assert it. We take it for granted, and what we take for granted we never take seriously. We need an outbreak of New Testament Christianity that will make an impact and create a commotion and precipitate a crisis. Let us just be Christians and we will make a head-on collision with this pagan world order in true Acts-of-the-Apostles style. The lines are drawn to-day between brethren in Christ and comrades in Antichrist. Called to be Christians, suffering as Christians, persuading others to be Christians, let us really be Christians or take down our sign.

XIV

"FORGET NOT ALL HIS BENEFITS"

LOOKING BACK across the years, I would say with the Psalmist, "Come and hear, all ye that fear God, and I will declare what he hath done for my soul." I cannot count my blessings nor name them one by one, but I am constantly being surprised at what the Lord has done. I have already enjoyed far more than I expected a few years ago. I can truly say that God has given me the desires of my heart.

I thank God for America. I would not want to be a man "with soul so dead who never to himself hath said, 'This is my own, my native land.'" We are infected to-day with a brand of pests who pretend to like it better the way they do it elsewhere. Some of us would gladly see them take a boat to-morrow for the land of their dreams if they don't like it here.

I am thankful for "Dixie-land, where I was born early on a frosty mornin'." I lived for five years in the heart of the Old South in Charleston, South Carolina. I know the jokes they tell on us Southerners, how we still fight the War Between the States. I trust I may not be accused of sectionalism, but I still like it best 'way down South.

I thank God that I grew up in the country, "far from

the madding crowd's ignoble strife." God made the country and man made the town—and you certainly can see the difference! A country boy may learn city ways but a city boy cannot learn country ways—you have to be born and grow up in the country to be natural. Someone has said that city people and country folks are just ignorant on different subjects. I am grateful for memories of cotton fields and watermelon patches, for the oak trees in the front yard and the honeysuckle vine on the back porch, for the mocking-bird in the morning, the wood thrush at sundown, and the whip-poor-will in the lone dark hills at night. I can still hear the night-hawk zooming in the evening summer sky, the crickets across the road, and the hoot owl in the deep woods giving me the shivers as I sat on the back porch pretending to wash my stub-toed feet before I went to bed. I thank God for the snowy world of winter and the miracle of spring, the good old summer time, and the tender wistfulness of autumn, "when the frost is on the 'punkin' and the fodder's in the shock." Often I have thought that if this world, marred and spoiled by sin, can be so lovely, what will the new earth be like when God has freed it from dictators, disease, death, and the devil and filled it with His glory as the waters cover the sea.

I am thankful for having had a Christian home. My parents took life seriously. Life was real and earnest, and the grave was not the goal. Father believed we came from somewhere and were going somewhere. There were foes to face and a flood to stem, and this poor world was no friend of grace to help us on to God. Like Noah, father got his family into the ark. I used to think he was a bit too strict, but I can see the point now. He could have compromised a little here and hedged a little there and dropped to the level of the average. He could have decided that maybe he was overdoing it and hidden behind the verse, "Be not righteous overmuch." But he was out to build with gold, silver, and precious stones and would not be inveigled into trafficking with wood, hay, and stubble. His life will stand the fire test, for he built soundly and managed to get some solid materials into the lives of his children as well.

I thank God for an experience of grace, which I have related elsewhere, and along with it a call to preach. I have enjoyed preaching. It may be misery to some, but I have not found it so. There are indeed ambassadors in bonds which they themselves have forged. Of course, if you are going to preach with one eye on a contrary deacon, if you are going to spend your time tickling the ears of a generation that cannot endure sound doctrine, if you are going to get your sermons from minister's manuals instead of digging into God's own storehouse as God's householder should do, if you are going to be that kind of preacher, you will never have liberty. No man can preach if he confers with flesh and blood for his authority. Let him go to Arabia and get his credentials from heaven. Let him shun Saul's armour and go after Goliath in his own native fashion and in the Name of the Lord. Blessed is God's ambassador who is not in bonds—bonds of habit, shackling sins of flesh or spirit, bonds within or bonds without, in his own family or church or among the ecclesiastics over him, bonds that quench the Spirit and stifle his message until he is a parrot instead of a prophet. Better live in the woods, eat berries, and drink spring water and keep one's own soul. We are in appalling need to-day of men who speak for God. Satan will try to scare any man who aspires to such a holy office. He hates a Micaiah who speaks only "what the Lord saith." He would make Baruchs of us all, feathering our nest in a world on fire. This is no time to hang up our stockings for the Santa Claus of this age to fill. Gehazi is all too prone to chase Naaman for a rake-off and bring upon himself the leprosy of God's judgement.

I thank God for friends, a host of them, whose prayers and provision have backed me up through the years. Their homes all over the land have opened to me. They have encouraged me and sometimes they have reproved, and I trust I have received both with appropriate grace. They listen to my sermons and read my books and bid me Godspeed. Many of them I have never seen, but we are bound together by the tie invisible. Eventually, many of us will meet for the first time, and in Christ we are always sure that Christians never meet for the last time!

But, above all, "thanks be unto God for his unspeakable gift." Charles Kingsley, when he was asked what was the secret of his beautiful life, answered, "I had a

friend." If my life ever approaches the beautiful it will
be because

> "I've found a Friend, O such a Friend!
> He loved me ere I knew Him;
> He drew me with the cords of love,
> And thus He bound me to Him."

Two boats passed each other on the Mississippi one
day, when an old coloured workman on one pointed to
the other boat and said to a white passenger beside him,
"Look, there's the captain! Years ago, we were going
along like this when I fell overboard and the captain
rescued me. And ever since then I just loves to point
him out!"

Once I was in waters too deep for my wit and will
to navigate, but the Captain of my salvation leaped
overboard and came from heaven to earth to rescue me.

And since then I just love to point Him out.

XV

"LORD, I BELIEVE . . ."

A CREED HAS been defined as "a half-way station between the Bible and the heart." Yet almost everyone who would press on in things spiritual sooner or later finds himself setting down his innermost convictions or reducing his covenant with God to writing.

For years I was continually writing down new resolutions, new statements of faith, going back to Bethel and recording it on paper. I carried these credos with me to read once in a while when the glory grew dim. But in recent years I have not been given to that procedure. For one thing, I observed that I overdid it, always trying to build tabernacles to house each mountain-top experience. I learned that while the glamour of such days always fades, we have Christ with us always and to cultivate His fellowship is far better than to try to maintain the glow of past exaltations.

But I needed not to spend time drawing up new declarations of faith, because, shortly after I came back to preaching the old message, I set down a few simple sentences which I have not found it necessary to amend or revise. Perhaps they will help someone else to crystallize his experience. At the first of every year, I simply enter them in my new notebook. They run as follows:

"I am trusting the Lord Jesus Christ as my Saviour." "Trusting" says it better than "believing." "Believing" may mean mere head knowledge to some, but to "trust" is to "stretch out upon," to repose in quiet dependence. And then, He is Saviour, not just an example, and "my Saviour," which makes it personal.

There was a time when I was troubled about assurance, the witness of the Spirit, the consciousness of sins forgiven and of my acceptance before God. I came to rest solely on what God had said in His Word. I never could feel as I thought I should feel. I couldn't get my experience to suit me. But I came to see that God had spoken, and I stood on the text, "Let God be true but every man a liar."

I was helped much by reading the experiences of others. Dr. R. W. Dale was troubled in his youth over whether he had the right kind of faith or not. But he gradually ceased to think of himself and became occupied with Christ. Then he was surprised to think that he had ever doubted.

Alexander McLaren's sermon on "The Witness of the Spirit" helped me greatly. And I treasure part of a letter from Alexander Whyte to a troubled soul:

"Draw nigh to God and He will draw nigh to you. Act faith if you do not feel it. . . . Christ is before you to take freely: accept Him, trust Him, believe what He says, assume that you are His and believe as if you were. Throw yourself in His direction even though you cannot reach Him. Even if you die doing this, He will take care of you. He does not say 'See,' He only says 'Look'; that is all you have to do, He will take care of the rest. . . . Many a time I feel so cold and dead that I might doubt if I had ever come to Him at all; but I go about my work notwithstanding, looking in His direction, and my heart fills by and by with His love to me. It was many years before I was aware that I was over the boundary line. It is very simple: keep looking, He will take care of the seeing."

"I yield to Jesus Christ all I am and have, and believe He has sanctified me and mine to His use and glory." There must be a complete committal of person and possessions. I like "committal" better than "surrender," for we surrender to an enemy but commit to a friend. By "sanctified" I do not mean some strange emotional experience but being set apart to God's use and glory. It must be to His use. There is no use praying, "Use me." He will use us if we are usable. He'll wear us out! And it must be to His glory. "Glorify thy name" was the Saviour's prayer, and it must be ours.

"I receive by faith the filling of the Spirit that I may glorify the Lord Jesus Christ in my life and testimony." I have related elsewhere my experience in this matter. There need to be refillings on special occasions. There is a gradual daily growth in grace, but there are special crises that demand special unction. Our Lord lived always in the will of the Father, but on certain occasions He prayed all night.

We are Spirit-filled that we may glorify Christ. "The

Holy Ghost was not yet given; because that Jesus was not yet glorified." That, of course, has another, a primary meaning, but it is also true that the Spirit is not given to us individually until we seek only to glorify Christ. F. B. Meyer warned us to beware of any movement that makes the Holy Spirit the figurehead. The Spirit bears witness to Jesus, and when people major on an experience or even the work of the Spirit instead of glorifying Christ, something is wrong. "Ye shall receive power . . . ye shall be witnesses unto me," that is the Divine order.

"Looking unto Jesus for every need, health, guidance, calls, results, funds, everything, I would know Him and make Him known in a life of faith working by love, and a ministry of 'Christ himself.'" I know that there have been many differences among Christians on the matter of healing. Perhaps A. T. Pierson summed it up as well as any:

"I say to you with the solemnity of a dying man that no man has ever yet laid hold of the supernatural power of God as it is possible for Him to lay hold of that power. God's great plan for human life is that the Holy Spirit entering into man's spirit shall transform man's convictions, his emotions, his sensibilities, his resolutions and even his body. I do not say that all disease is a direct result of sin, but I am bold to say that we know very little of what the power of God means in transforming disposition and intellect and conduct, and we have still less conception of what blessing might come even to the bodies of saints if, with apostolic faith, apostolic power returned to the church."

I do know that Christ is our life and according to the faith we have we are to trust Him to sustain even our bodies and rest assured that He will keep us here as long as He wants us in this world, for "we are immortal until our work is done."

"Guidance." "In all thy ways acknowledge Him and He shall direct thy paths." It is easier to preach about guidance than to be sure of it in some cases. Sometimes we expect the Lord to make it plainer than He does. By the Word, prayer, meditation, circumstances, sometimes the advice of true Christian friends, by steps and by stops, "God leads His dear children along."

"Calls, results, funds." I have found it best to let the Lord open doors without any effort on my part. Sometimes I have become too anxious when there was no visible response to my preaching and unduly elated when there was. Homer Hammontree tells of his days with Dr. Torrey and of how the great evangelist was not upset when there was apparent failure and was not elated when there was great success. "The wind bloweth where it listeth," and it is not possible to determine fully which meeting is the greater defeat or victory. And God has provided finances according to His gracious promise to meet all our needs. I have never felt that a minister should set a price for his services. I cannot imagine Paul saying, "I will come over to Macedonia for a thousand dollars and expenses." Sam Jones used to say God would feed a Christian if he had to put the angels on half rations.

"My citizenship is in heaven; from whence also we

look for the Saviour, the Lord Jesus Christ. Even so, come, Lord Jesus." I am a citizen of heaven sojourning on earth, not a citizen of earth journeying to heaven. God help me never to lose my pilgrim character. It is so easy to drive down our tent-pegs in this world. I would sit loose to its attractions like the coloured mammy who said, "I wears dis world like a loose garment."

I am not merely looking for something to happen but for Someone to come. When I studied arithmetic, I remembered that the answers were in the back of the book. No matter how I floundered among my problems, the correct solution was on the last page. I have failed often in working out life's problems, and I dwell in the midst of a people who are hopelessly trying to untangle the riddle of this present age. But I am cheered by one unfailing certainty—there is a Book that solves the enigma and the answer is in the back of the Book, "Behold I come quickly." "Even so, come, Lord Jesus."

Dover Memorial Library
Gardner-Webb University
P.O. Box 836
Boiling Springs, N.C. 28017

Havner, Vance, 1901-
"That I may know Him," a
personal testimony.